MONSTERS from the DEEP

Charlotte Raby

OXFORD
UNIVERSITY PRESS

OXFORD
UNIVERSITY PRESS

is a department of the University of Oxford.
It furthers the University's objective of excellence in research, scholarship,
and education by publishing worldwide in

Oxford   New York

Auckland   Cape Town   Dar es Salaam   Hong Kong   Karachi
Kuala Lumpur   Madrid   Melbourne   Mexico City   Nairobi
New Delhi   Shanghai   Taipei   Toronto

With offices in

Argentina   Austria   Brazil   Chile   Czech Republic   France   Greece
Guatemala   Hungary   Italy   Japan   Poland   Portugal   Singapore
South Korea   Switzerland   Thailand   Turkey   Ukraine   Vietnam

Database right Oxford University Press (maker)

First published 2007

British Library Cataloguing in Publication Data

Data available

ISBN: 978-0-19-846115-9

9 10 8

Printed in China

Paper used in the production of this book is a natural,
recyclable product made from wood grown in sustainable forests.
The manufacturing process conforms to the environmental
regulations of the country of origin

Acknowledgements

The publisher would like to thank the following for permission to reproduce photographs: **p4**l David
Fleetham/Photolibrary Group, **p4**r AKG – Images; **p5**t Peter David/Natural Visions, **p5**b Ralph White/
Corbis UK Ltd.; **p6** Silvia Hertig/Archaeological Institute/University of Zurich; **p10** Mary Evans Picture
Library; **p11**t AKG – Images, **p11**c Mary Evans Picture Library, **p11**b Mary Evans Picture Library/Alamy;
p13t Associated Press/Empics, **p13**b Norbert Wu/NHPA; **p14** Mark Mitchell/Rex Features; **p15**tl Mark
Mitchell/Rex Features, **p15**tr Ian Nicholson/PA Wire/Empics, **p15**b Sinclair Stammers/Science Photo
Library; **p16** Jerry Choi/Alamy; **p18** Toru Yamanaka/AFP/Getty Images; **p21**t Natural History Museum,
p21b Ralph White/Corbis UK Ltd

Cover photograph: Corbis

Illustrations by: Julian Baker: **p20**; Brett Breckon; **p14**, **p16**, **p19**, **p22**, **p23**; Martin Sanders/
Beehive Illustration: **p8/9**, **p17**; Lazlo Veres/Beehive Illustration: **p6**, **p7**, **p8/9** (insets)

Contents

Where do sea monsters come from?

The seas are a mystery.
Ever since people could sail, they
have been amazed at the creatures
that appear from its depths. Some
creatures are too fabulous to
imagine, like flying fish. Some are
terrible and terrifying.

Scientific discoveries

Sailors' stories, and actual sea creatures they brought back, made some scientists want to learn more. They joined sailors on their voyages to see the creatures first-hand. Amazing discoveries were made and the scientists realized that the seas held countless creatures.

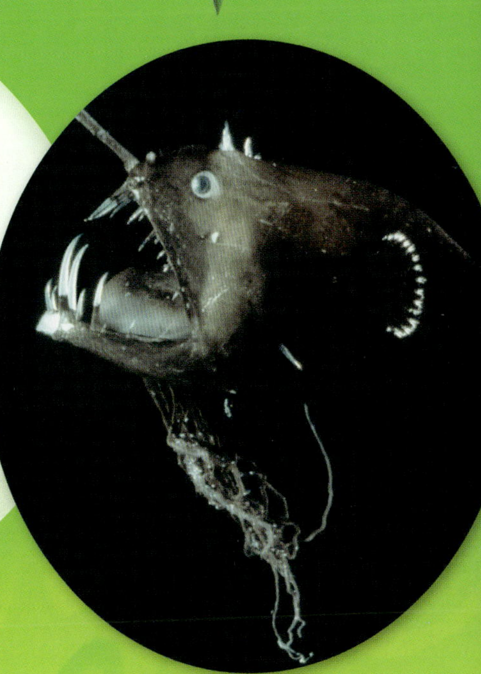

Could sea monsters be real?

Although we now have submarines that reach great depths, we still haven't explored every part of the oceans. Scientists say that they expect to continue to discover new creatures for many years to come. Some of the creatures may even be the incredible monsters described in this book.

In this book you will explore:
- **living fossils**
- newly discovered sea animals
- incredible creatures
- some amazing monsters!

Sea myths and legends

1500 BC
Greeks

AD 420–588
Liang Dynasty, China

AD 730–1066
Norse

Sea-monster stories are ancient. There are sea monsters in Greek myths, Norse legends and ancient stories from China and the Americas.

Greek sea monsters

The Ketos were shark-monsters. They appear in Greek myths as servants to the sea god, Poseidon. In one myth, Poseidon sent a Ketos to terrorize the city of Troy. **Heracles** saved the city by killing the monster.

This Greek pot shows Heracles fighting a Ketos.

The Norse Kraken

The Norse people were fearless sailors who set sail into the seas' wildest reaches. The most famous Norse sea-monster story is about the kraken. This creature was said to attack ships using its many arms to **capsize** them. Over two thousand years later, sailors still fear the dreadful kraken.

Chinese and Canadian water dragons

There are tales of water dragons in many countries. The people of China and Canada have told ancient tales of these monsters going back 2,500 years. Both countries' legends say that the dragons need people to honour them. The Chinese hold boat races and native Canadians give dragon offerings.

Early sea voyages

If you have been lucky enough to sail in a small boat or canoe you can imagine what early seafarers must have felt.

Native American canoe – North-West Pacific coast

Aztec dugout canoe

The earliest sailors voyaged in small boats. The people of Australasia and the Americas used dugout canoes and **double-hulled** rafts to make long sea journeys.

The Norse had rowing boats called long boats that journeyed all the way to Iceland and Greenland (see the route on the map).

These brave people set out to explore the unknown. They battled against huge waves in their small boats. They also encountered strange creatures and were perhaps the first people to see whales, squid, octopus and flying fish.

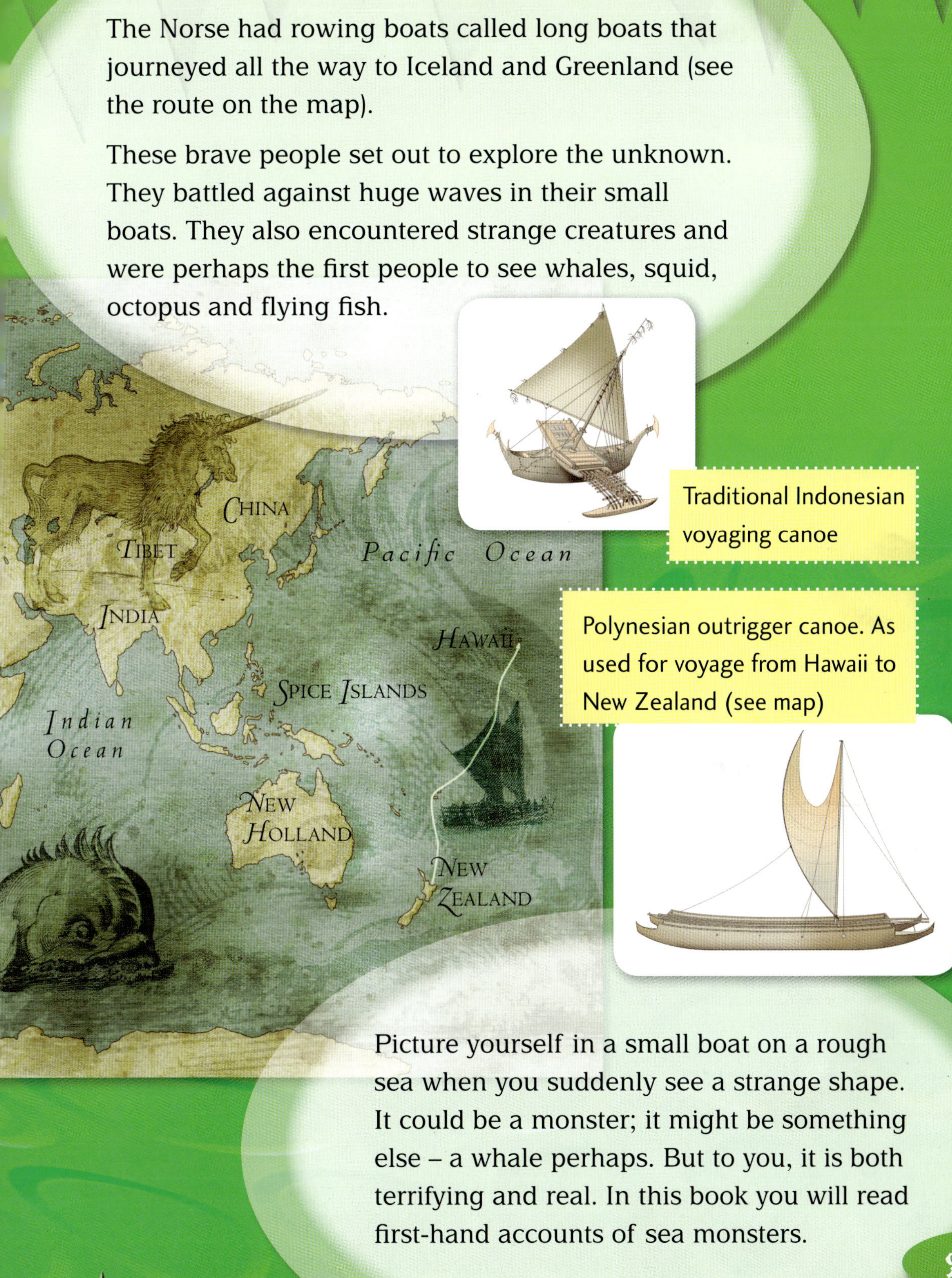

Traditional Indonesian voyaging canoe

Polynesian outrigger canoe. As used for voyage from Hawaii to New Zealand (see map)

Picture yourself in a small boat on a rough sea when you suddenly see a strange shape. It could be a monster; it might be something else – a whale perhaps. But to you, it is both terrifying and real. In this book you will read first-hand accounts of sea monsters.

Four monsters

Imagine travelling further than any human ever has, through an ever-changing landscape. Now imagine seeing creatures so weird and strange that you cannot find the words to describe them.

The following four monsters were drawn from sightings by early sea travellers. All of them look strange and frightening. However, if we look carefully perhaps we can work out which sea creatures they really are.

A scientist drew this in 1764. He thought the sailor had described a hydra, a monster found in Greek myths. Imagine that the snake-like heads are tentacles. Could this be an octopus?

Look closely at this creature with its shaggy mane, fat body and clawed feet. Could this be a walrus?

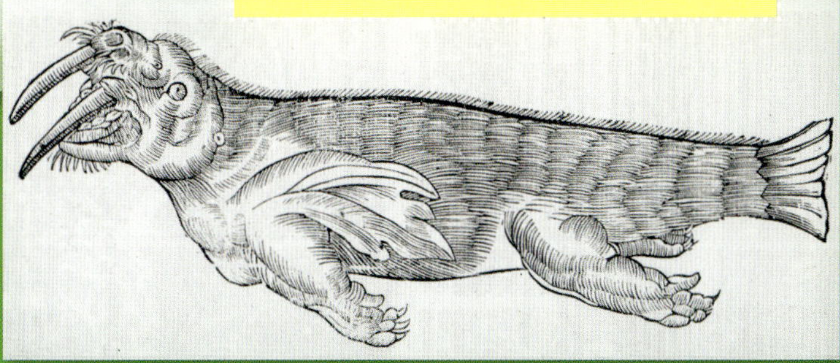

This drawing entitled 'Bearded Whale' was drawn in 1558.

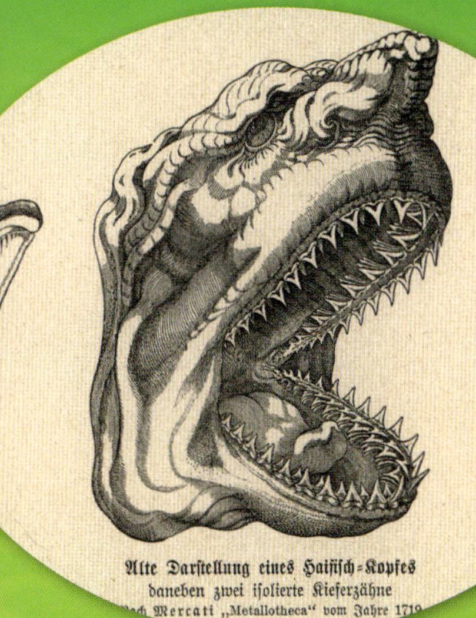

What a terrible monster! In fact, it is a **decayed** shark's head. As sailors couldn't freeze the sea creatures they found, scientists were often given rotting animals to look at.

The head of a giant white shark, drawn in 1719.

This monster appeared to be the length of a ship and was seen snorting out water. Was it a whale?

A sea monster, spotted and drawn by Hans Egede on 6 July 1734.

11

Curse of the sea serpent

Hundreds of people say they have seen sea serpents. Could sea serpents really exist? Look at the descriptions below before you make up your mind.

Two English scientists saw a sea serpent in Brazil in 1905.

The crew of the *HMS Daedulus* watched the sea serpent near the Cape of Good Hope in 1848.

In 1966, Captain John Ridgway thought he saw a sea serpent in the Atlantic Ocean.

Oarfish – Is this the monster?

This picture is of a giant oarfish. They are very rare creatures and can grow to a massive 15 metres in length. This huge fish is less than half that size!

A gigantic oarfish, caught in 1954 in Sydney, Australia

Underwater cameraman John Bird saw an oarfish in the wild. John says, "The creature had a large **plume** of strands on its head pointing upwards." Could it be the sea serpent?

Squid vision

What are squid?

Squids are soft-bodied **marine** creatures. They are **carnivores** that eat sea worms, fish and smaller squid.

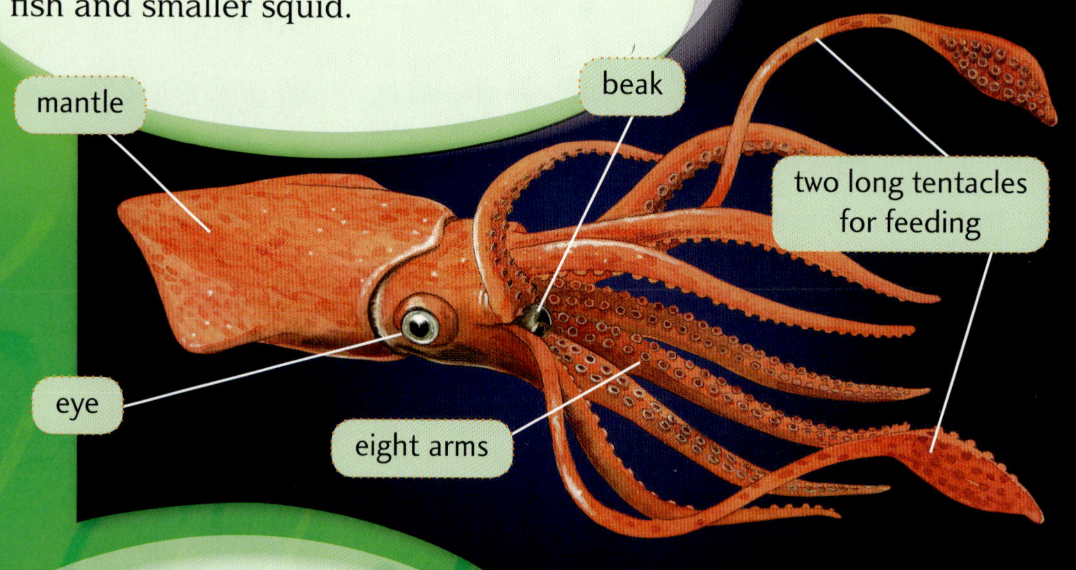

Everyone thought the biggest squid was the giant squid. It measures up to 18 metres long, which is twice as big as a bus.

In 2003, fishermen in New Zealand discovered a new **species** of squid. They found the squid attacking fish they had caught in their nets. The squid was so big that it became known as a 'colossal squid'.

This colossal squid is not a fully-grown adult. Scientists believe they grow up to 25m long.

Super squid facts

The squid has the largest eye of any animal.

Sperm whales hunt the giant and colossal squid. The squids defend themselves by using weapons on their tentacles. The battles must be fierce because whales have been found with cuts caused by squids.

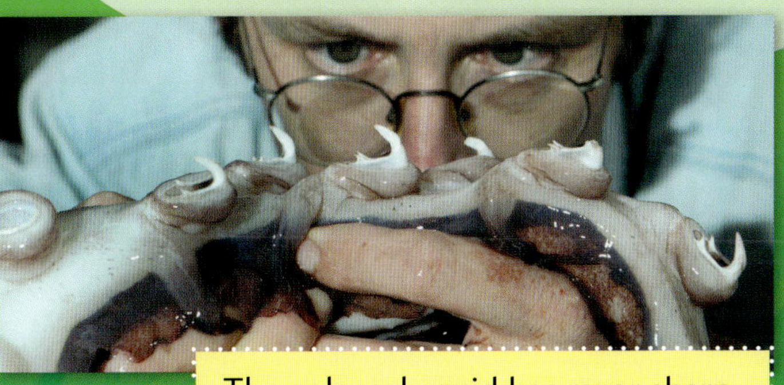

The colossal squid has razor-sharp hooks to shred its **prey**.

The giant squid has circular saw-like sucker rings.

Squids use large, sharp beaks inside their mouths for feeding.

The giant and colossal squids live at depths of about 2000 metres in the freezing waters of the Antarctic. This is why they have been so hard to find and study.

Imagine a crab that grows as big as a small car. The giant Japanese crab grows up to 4 metres long, measured from claw to claw. You wouldn't like to find this crab at the end of your foot!

The giant Japanese crab stands on its long legs to make it look even bigger.

Fact file – the giant Japanese crab

What type of crab is it?

A spider crab.

Where is it found?

In the Pacific Ocean near Japan.

Where is its home?

In holes in the ocean floor at depths of 50–300 metres.

What does it eat?

Shellfish and dead sea creatures.

Who are its enemies?

The octopus.

How does it protect itself?

This is a pretty tough crab. The massive pincers give a really nasty nip. Giant crabs also use **camouflage**; they cover themselves in sponges and other animals to make them look like part of the ocean floor.

How long does it live?

Up to a hundred years.

Megamouth shark – a living fossil

Have you ever wondered what it would be like to come face to face with a dinosaur? Well it has happened! Animals that scientists thought were extinct for millions of years have suddenly been found. They are called living fossils.

The megamouth shark is a living fossil. It is so rare that in the 30 years since its discovery only 36 have been found.

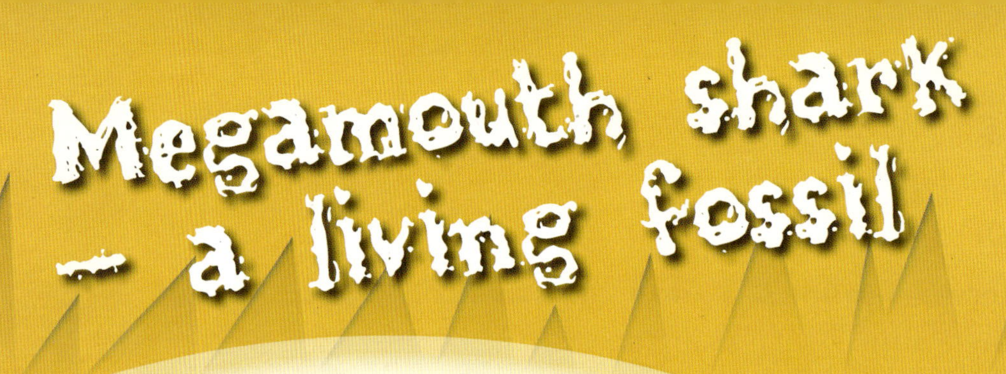

The megamouth shark has a huge mouth but tiny teeth. It only eats **plankton** and jellyfish.

Is the megamouth a monster?

This shark isn't a monster but it is the key to a mystery. It is a **primitive** shark and by looking at it we can imagine how sharks have changed. It helps us to understand what the sea was like millions of years ago when enormous sharks such as Carcharodon megalodon existed.

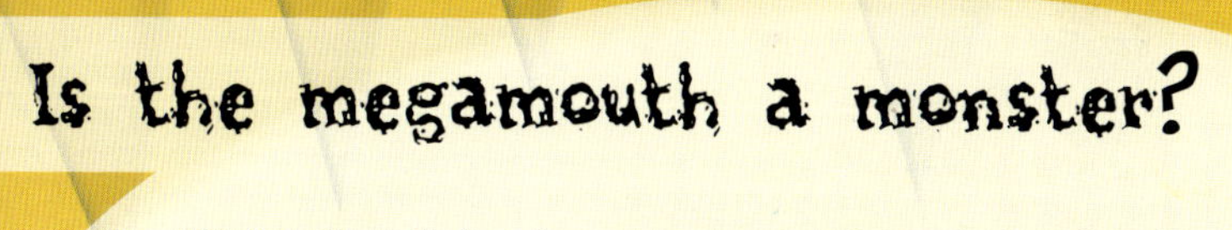

You can see a video of a megamouth in the wild at http://www.arkive.org/. Put 'megamouth shark' in the Advanced Search box, select 'Movies', click on the 'Megamouth shark' movie and be prepared to be amazed!

The Marine Times

16 July, 2003

New Deep Hole Discovered

A new 'hole' in the **Marianas Trench** has been found. Scientists believe the trench called HMRG Deep may be even deeper than Challenger Deep.

Challenger Deep, which was discovered in 1951, but which has only recently been measured, is known to be 11 kilometres deep. That means you could fit the whole of Mount Everest in the trench and still have 1.6 kilometres of water above it!

With only 1 per cent of the oceans' floor explored, scientists expect to find incredible marine life inside this trench.

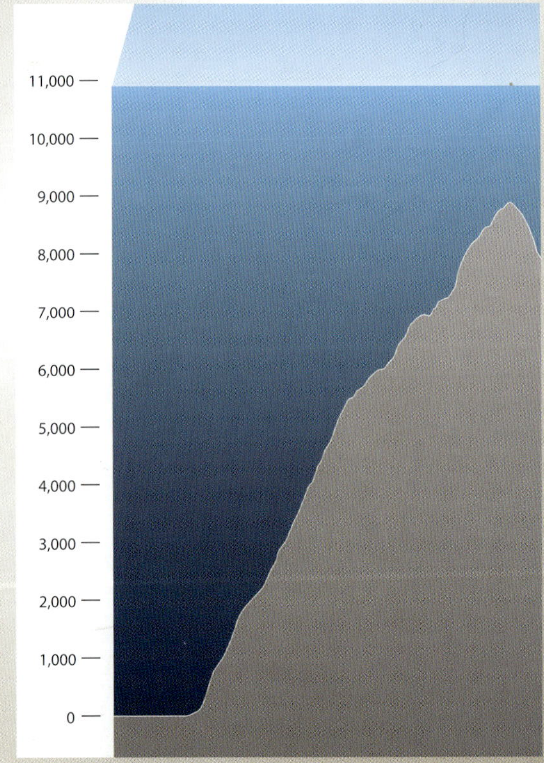

The world's biggest mountain easily fits in the sea's deepest trench.

18 October, 2005

Whales' graveyard

Dead whales or 'whale falls' are home to many specialist marine creatures. Scientists have discovered that when dead whales fall to the ocean floor they take many years to decay. 'Whale falls' become home to an **ecosystem** of marine life, such as bone-eating 'zombie worms' and hag fish.

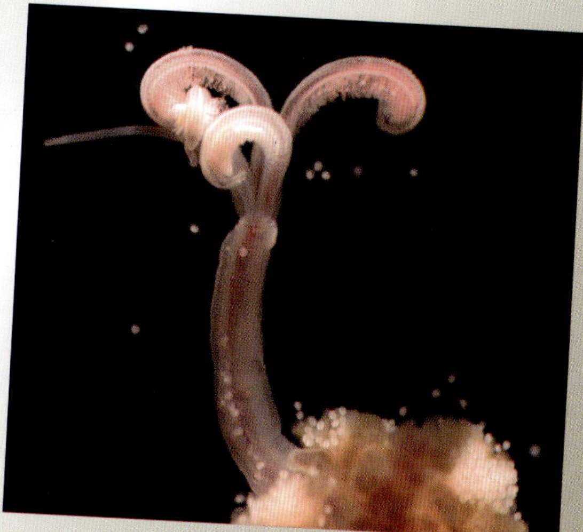

This worm was found in a minke whale bone.

16 July, 2003

THERE ARE GIANTS DEEP DOWN

We knew there were giant crabs, squid and octopus. Now there is a new giant: a tube worm measuring 2 metres in length has been found on the ocean's floor. These strange worms are only found on super-heated vents made by undersea volcanoes. This is because the vents make chemicals that the tube worms feed on.

Giant tube worms are found at depths of at least 1.5 kilometres.

Super sea monster

We have looked at some strange and amazing creatures in this book. Sometimes reality is stranger than fiction. Are the two real sea monsters stronger, cleverer or scarier than the two fictional sea monsters? Which is the super sea monster? You decide.

Colossal squid

Habitat: 2000 metres (that's 2 kilometres) deep, in the Antarctic Ocean

Size: 25 metres long

Weight: up to 1 tonne

Meetings with people: only just discovered; it was very aggressive

Special features: the biggest eye in the world and razor-sharp swivel hooks on its tentacles

Speed: this squid really moves – it gets chased by whales, which can travel at 43 kilometres per hour

Kraken

Habitat: deep cold water

Size: so large it has been mistaken for an island

Weight: unknown

Meetings with people: many; from AD 850 to the 1930s kraken have attacked ships

Special features: enormous tentacles that can wrap around a boat

Speed: unbelievable speed (and strength)

Giant Japanese crab

Habitat: 50–300 metres deep, in the Pacific Ocean

Size: 4 metres

Weight: 20 kilograms

Meetings with people: this giant is a Japanese delicacy and is caught to eat!

Special features: ten jointed legs, two with very large pincers

Speed: very slow

Sea serpent

Habitat: warm seas around the Americas and Indian Ocean

Size: up to 60 metres

Weight: unknown

Meetings with people: observed by sailors, but no attacks have been reported

Special features: able to wrap itself around whales

Speed: speedy

Glossary

camouflage – the way an animal's colour or shape helps it blend into its surroundings

capsize – when a boat turns over in the water

carnivores – living things that eat other animals

decayed – the way something rots once it is dead

double-hulled – to have two hulls (a boat's hull is the bottom part that goes in the water)

ecosystem – all the plants and creatures living together in an area

encountered – had nasty or difficult meetings

fossil – the remains of an animal or a plant, which have gradually turned into rock

Heracles (Hercules) – an Ancient Greek and Roman hero

living fossil – an animal or plant thought to be extinct, but then discovered living and in its original form

Marianas Trench – the deepest part of the Earth's oceans

marine – connected to the sea

plume – a decorative group of feathers

plankton – very small forms of plant and animal life that live in water

prey – an animal or a bird that is hunted, killed and eaten by another

primitive – in the early stages of development for its species

species – groups of related living things

Index